Book #1: Pre Campaign Planning

Vince Casale

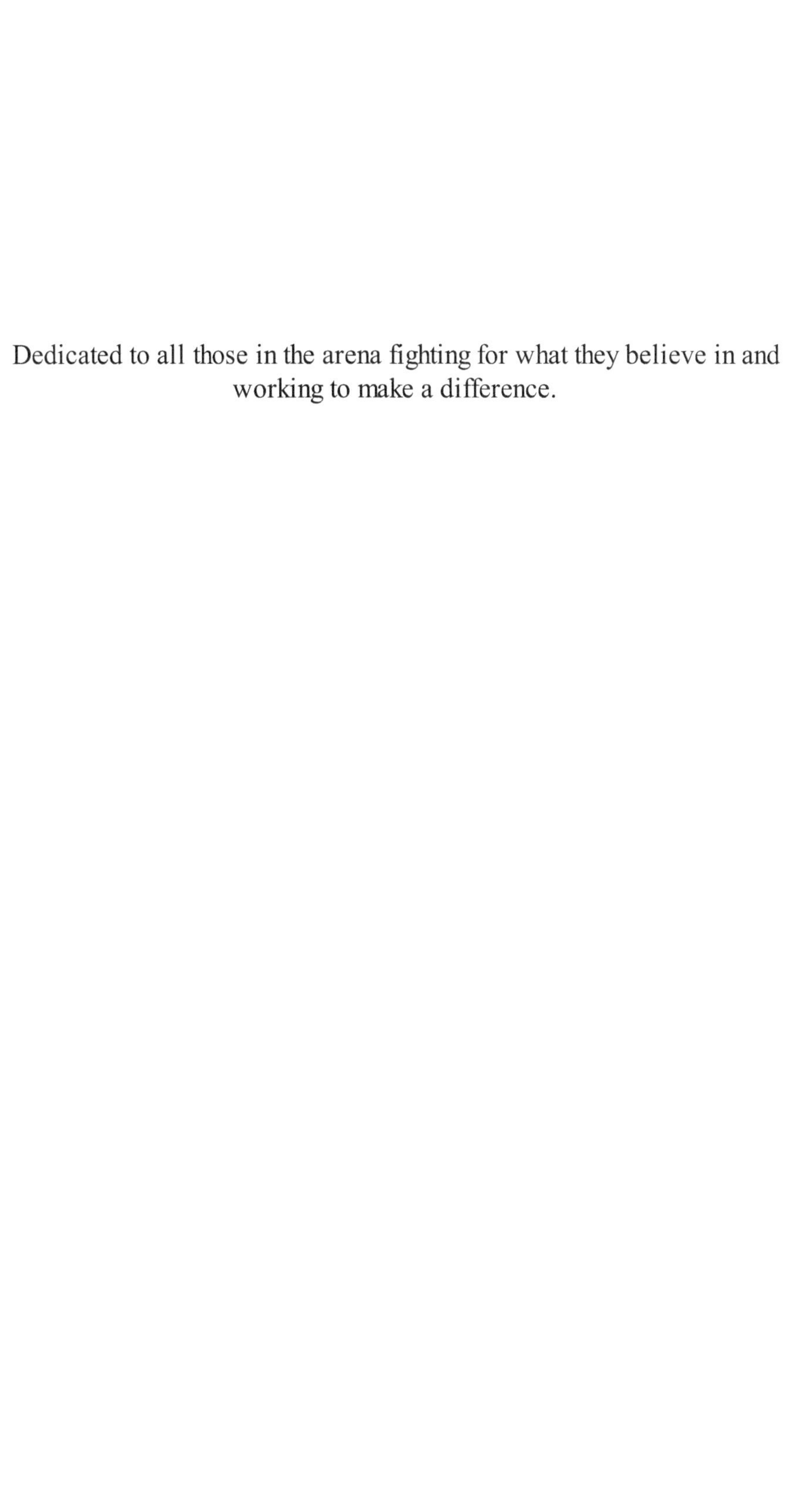

Dedicated to all those in the arena fighting for what they believe in and working to make a difference.

INTRODUCTION

WELCOME TO THE first book in the 50 Plus 1 series, where you will learn how to plan and run a successful political campaign. But first, let's start with the meaning behind the title "50 Plus 1." In most elections, the candidate who receives 50% of the votes plus one additional vote wins the election. Hence, "50 Plus 1" is the magical number that can secure your victory.

This book will guide you through the pre-campaign planning stage, which is crucial for laying the foundation of your campaign. You'll learn how to understand the political landscape, define your goals and objectives, develop a campaign message, identify your target audience, conduct market research, and petition to get on the ballot.

CHAPTER ONE

Understanding the Political Landscape

POLITICS CAN BE a confusing and complex world, but in order to run a successful campaign, it's important to have a clear understanding of the political landscape. In this chapter, we'll explore the different levels of government, the electoral process, the various players involved in politics, and how different political issues can impact the landscape.

Levels of Government

The United States has three levels of government: federal, state, and local. Each level of government has its own set of elected officials and responsibilities. Federal government deals with national issues such as foreign policy, national defense, and interstate commerce. State governments have the power to legislate on matters within their own borders, while local governments handle issues within their own communities such as zoning, policing, and education.

The Electoral Process

In the United States, elections are held at all levels of government. Federal elections are held every two years for the House of Representatives and every six years for the Senate. The President is elected every four years. State and local elections are held on a variety of schedules, depending on the specific jurisdiction.

Campaigns and Candidates

Campaigns are the organized efforts to promote a particular candidate or issue. Candidates are individuals who are seeking to be elected to public office. Campaigns can be run by individuals, political parties, or interest groups.

In order to be a successful candidate, you must understand the issues that matter to voters and have a clear message about how you plan to address those issues. You also need to have a solid understanding of the electorate and the voting process. This means understanding how different demographic groups are likely to vote and what issues are most important to them.

Political Issues

Political issues are the concerns and problems that are important to voters and can shape the political landscape. Examples of political issues include healthcare, immigration, gun control, taxes, and the environment. These issues can be divided into different categories such as social issues, economic issues, and foreign policy issues.

Social issues include topics such as abortion, civil rights, and LGBTQ rights. Economic issues include topics such as jobs, taxes, and the minimum wage. Foreign policy issues include topics such as trade, national security, and international relations.

The impact of political issues on the political landscape can vary depending on the issue and the election. For example, in a presidential election, foreign policy issues may receive more attention than social issues, while in a midterm election, economic issues may be more important.

To better understand the political issues that are important to the voters in your district or region, it is essential to conduct thorough research. Start by reviewing the latest news stories and reports from reputable sources. Attend town hall meetings, community forums, and other local events where you can interact with voters and learn more about their concerns. Additionally, reach out to local political groups and community leaders to get a sense of the political climate and key issues. Don't be afraid to ask questions and listen carefully to the responses. By understanding the political landscape and the issues that matter most to voters, you can tailor your campaign message and platform to resonate with your target audience.

Conclusion

Understanding the political landscape and the various issues that impact it is a crucial first step in running a successful campaign. In this chapter, we've covered the levels of government, the electoral process, the key players involved in politics, and how political issues can shape the landscape. In the next chapter, we'll dive into how to define your goals and objectives for your campaign. But before we move on, take a few minutes to complete the worksheet at the end of this chapter to assess your understanding of the political landscape and identify any areas where you may need to do further research.

CHAPTER TWO

Defining Your Goals and Objectives

ONE OF THE most important steps in running a successful political campaign is to define your goals and objectives. This involves identifying what you want to achieve and how you plan to achieve it. Without clear goals and objectives, your campaign may lack direction and fail to connect with voters.

To begin, think about what you hope to accomplish with your campaign. Are you running for office to enact change in a particular area of policy? Or are you hoping to represent a particular constituency that has been underrepresented in the political sphere? Whatever your goals may be, it is important to define them clearly and communicate them effectively to your team and potential supporters.

It is also important to set measurable objectives that will help you track your progress and determine whether you are on track to achieve your goals. For example, if you are running for city council with the goal of improving public transportation, a measurable objective might be to increase public transportation usage by 10% within the first year of your term.

When setting your goals and objectives, it is important to keep your target audience in mind. What issues are most important to the voters in your district? How can you connect with them and communicate your message effectively? By tailoring your goals and objectives to the needs and concerns of your target audience, you can increase your chances of success.

Here's an example: Let's say you are running for school board and your goal is to improve the quality of education in your district. Your objectives might include improving teacher retention rates, increasing student test scores, and increasing parent engagement in the educational process. By setting measurable objectives in each of these areas, you can track your progress and adjust your campaign strategy as needed.

In summary, defining clear and measurable goals and objectives is essential for a successful political campaign. By keeping your target audience in mind and tailoring your goals and objectives to their needs and concerns, you can increase your chances of success.

CHAPTER THREE

Developing a Campaign Message

ONE OF THE most important aspects of any political campaign is developing a clear and concise campaign message that resonates with voters. Your message should be easy to understand and memorable, while also highlighting your strengths and setting you apart from your opponents.

To begin developing your message, start by asking yourself some key questions: What issues do you care about? What do you stand for? What makes you unique?

Once you have a good understanding of your own values and goals, you can start to craft a message that speaks to your supporters.

Your message should be based on your campaign platform, which should be a set of policies and ideas that you want to promote if you are elected. Your platform should be based on the issues that matter most to your supporters and should be tailored to the specific needs of your community.

When developing your campaign message, consider the following tips:

1. Keep it simple: Your message should be easy to understand and remember. Avoid using complicated jargon or language that may confuse voters.

2. Make it emotional: People are more likely to remember a message that evokes emotion. Try to tap into the hopes and fears of your audience, and use language that creates a sense of urgency.
3. Use storytelling: People are more likely to remember a message that tells a story. Use anecdotes and examples to illustrate your points and make your message more relatable.
4. Highlight your strengths: Your message should focus on your strengths and what sets you apart from your opponents. Use language that highlights your unique qualities and accomplishments.
5. Be consistent: Your message should be consistent across all of your campaign materials, from your website to your campaign literature. This will help voters remember your message and associate it with your campaign.

For example, if you are running for city council and your platform focuses on improving local parks, your message might be something like: "I believe every family deserves a safe and beautiful place to play. As your city council member, I will fight to improve our local parks and ensure they are accessible to everyone."

Remember, your campaign message should be tailored to your specific audience and should be designed to resonate with the issues that matter most to them. By developing a clear and compelling message, you can set yourself apart from your opponents and build support among voters.

Campaign Slogan

Developing a memorable and effective campaign slogan is an important part of developing a campaign message. A good slogan should be catchy, easy to remember, and represent the candidate's values and platform. Here are some tips on developing a great campaign slogan:

1. Keep it simple: A slogan should be easy to remember and understand. Avoid using complicated jargon or language.
2. Make it memorable: A memorable slogan can help a candidate stand out in a crowded field. Use alliteration, rhyme, or repetition to make the

slogan catchy.

3. Highlight your strengths: A campaign slogan should focus on the candidate's strengths and what sets them apart from the competition. For example, "Stronger Together" was a memorable slogan used by Hillary Clinton during her 2016 presidential campaign.
4. Be positive: A positive campaign slogan is more likely to resonate with voters than a negative one. Avoid attacking opponents or using fear-mongering tactics.
5. Make it relevant: A campaign slogan should be relevant to the issues and concerns of voters. For example, during the 2020 US presidential campaign, Joe Biden used the slogan "Build Back Better" to highlight his plan to address the economic impact of the COVID-19 pandemic.

Some examples of successful campaign slogans include Barack Obama's "Yes We Can," Ronald Reagan's "Make America Great Again," and Donald Trump's "Keep America Great." These slogans were simple, memorable, and highlighted the candidates' strengths and values.

CHAPTER FOUR

Identifying Your Target Audience

ONE OF THE most important aspects of running a successful political campaign is identifying your target audience. This means understanding who your potential supporters are, what motivates them, and what issues they care about. Without a clear understanding of your target audience, your message is likely to fall on deaf ears.

The first step in identifying your target audience is to conduct research. This can include polling, focus groups, and data analysis. By gathering information about voters in your district or constituency, you can begin to build a profile of your target audience.

Once you have a sense of who your target audience is, you can tailor your message to their interests and concerns. For example, if you are running for city council and your research shows that your target audience is primarily concerned with traffic congestion and public transportation, you can emphasize your plans for improving public transportation and reducing traffic.

It's also important to consider the demographics of your target audience, such as age, gender, and race. For example, if you are running for office in a district with a large Hispanic population, you may want to consider running ads in Spanish and emphasizing your commitment to issues that are important to Hispanic voters.

In addition to demographics, you should also consider the values and beliefs of your target audience. For example, if you are running as a progressive candidate, you may want to emphasize your support for policies that promote social justice and equality.

Finally, it's important to remember that your target audience may change over the course of your campaign. As you gain momentum and attract new supporters, you may need to adjust your message to appeal to a broader audience.

Overall, identifying your target audience is a critical component of running a successful political campaign. By understanding who your potential supporters are and what motivates them, you can tailor your message and outreach efforts to maximize your impact.

CHAPTER FIVE

Conducting Market Research

IN ORDER TO run an effective political campaign, it's important to have a solid understanding of the people you're trying to reach. This means conducting market research to identify the wants, needs, and concerns of your target audience. Market research can help you develop a more effective campaign message, identify the issues that matter most to your audience, and tailor your outreach efforts to better connect with voters.

There are a few different methods you can use to conduct market research for your political campaign. One of the most common is polling, which involves surveying a representative sample of your target audience to gather information about their opinions, beliefs, and voting intentions. You can conduct polling through phone calls, online surveys, or in-person interviews.

Focus groups are another common market research method. A focus group is a moderated discussion with a small group of people who are part of your target audience. The moderator asks questions to the group, and the participants discuss their thoughts and opinions. Focus groups can provide valuable insights into how people feel about different issues, and can help you identify common concerns and themes.

Another way to conduct market research is through data analysis. This involves gathering and analyzing data about your target audience, such as voter registration records, demographic information, and voting patterns. You can also use data analysis to track social media engagement, website traffic, and other metrics to gauge the effectiveness of your outreach efforts.

Once you have gathered data through market research, it's important to analyze and interpret the results. Look for patterns and trends in the data to identify the key issues and concerns of your target audience. Use this information to refine your campaign message, tailor your outreach efforts, and develop a more effective overall campaign strategy.

For example, if your research shows that voters in your district are particularly concerned about access to affordable healthcare, you might focus your campaign message on your plans to increase access to healthcare services. If you find that voters in a certain neighborhood are more likely to engage with social media, you might focus your outreach efforts on those platforms.

In summary, conducting market research is a critical component of any successful political campaign. By gathering information about your target audience and analyzing the results, you can develop a more effective campaign message, tailor your outreach efforts, and ultimately connect with voters in a more meaningful way.

CHAPTER SIX

Political Petitioning to Get on the Ballot

GETTING YOUR NAME on the ballot is one of the most important steps in running a political campaign. For starters, it's crucial to understand the legal requirements for filling out petitions to ensure the process is valid and to avoid any issues or disqualifications.

In every state, there are specific laws regarding who is eligible to collect signatures, the form and format of the petition, and who can legally sign a specific petition. It's essential to research and follow these laws to ensure that your petitions are valid and accepted.

It's also recommended that you have a lawyer with knowledge of election law or someone with extensive experience overseeing the petitioning process to help guide and review your efforts. This can help ensure that all legal requirements are met and minimize the risk of disqualification due to errors or omissions.

Remember, ballot access requirements can differ from state to state, so it's essential to contact the relevant authority in your state or region who oversees elections to get specific information about the petitioning process.

Some states only require the filing of paperwork and the paying of a fee to access the ballot. If you are unsure of the process to get on the ballot in your state or municipality, now is a good time to find out before reading more about the petition process.

Petitioning requires collecting a certain number of signatures from registered voters in your district. The number of signatures required can vary depending on the office you are seeking and the area you are running in. It is essential to gather more signatures than required to account for invalid signatures or signatures that may be disqualified for some reason.

To start petitioning, you need to establish a team of dedicated volunteers who will collect signatures from registered voters in your district. You can also hire paid signature collectors if it is allowed in your area.

It is important to have clear instructions for your signature collectors and provide them with identification badges, clipboards, and pens. You should also give them a script to follow to ensure that they provide the correct information to potential signers.

When you are petitioning, stay organized and track your progress. You can use a spreadsheet or other tools to keep track of how many signatures you have collected and where they came from.

Also remember the petition process is a voter touch. Have a handout or placard available to leave with voters to learn more about you and your campaign. The list of voters who signed your petition can also be used later in your GOTV (Get Out The Vote) operation to ensure these early supporters to the polls.

Finally, it is crucial that the signatures you have collected meet the requirements set by the authority in charge of elections in your area. Make sure that the signatures are legible, that the signers are registered voters in your district, and that the signatures are dated within the allowed time frame.

Overall, petitioning can be a challenging but essential part of getting your name on the ballot. With careful planning, organization, and attention to detail, you can succeed in this critical step in your campaign.

CHAPTER SEVEN

Conclusion

IN CONCLUSION, UNDERSTANDING the political landscape, defining your goals and objectives, developing a campaign message, identifying your target audience, and conducting market research are all vital components of pre-campaign planning. By taking the time to carefully plan your campaign, you are setting yourself up for success.

To help you put everything you've learned in this book into action, we have designed a worksheet that will guide you through the process of pre-campaign planning. The worksheet will help you identify key aspects of your campaign, such as your goals and target audience, and allow you to create a comprehensive plan that will set you on the path to victory.

Remember, the key to a successful campaign is preparation. By putting in the time and effort to plan your campaign effectively, you are setting yourself up for success. We wish you the best of luck in your political endeavors and hope that this book has provided you with the tools you need to win.

So, take a deep breath, grab your worksheet, and start planning your winning campaign!

WORSHEET

50 PLUS 1
Pre-Campaign Planning Worksheet

Understanding the Political Landscape

- What are the top political issues that voters in my area care about?
- What are the strengths and weaknesses of my opponents?
- Who are the key political players in my area?

Defining Your Goals and Objectives

- What do I want to achieve in this campaign?
- What are my specific, measurable, attainable, relevant, and time-bound (SMART) goals?
- How will I measure the success of my campaign?

Developing a Campaign Message

- What is my campaign's central message?
- What specific policies or actions will I prioritize?
- How will I communicate my message to voters?

Identifying Your Target Audience

- Who are the voters I need to persuade to win?
- What are their demographics (age, gender, income, etc.)?
- What are their key concerns and priorities?

Conducting Market Research

- What data can I gather to inform my campaign strategy?
- What are the best ways to gather data (surveys, focus groups, etc.)?
- How will I analyze and use the data to inform my campaign?

Political Petitioning to Get on the Ballot

- What are the legal requirements and dates for ballot access in my state?
- Who is eligible to collect signatures and sign the petition?
- What steps will I take to ensure I have enough valid signatures?

By answering these questions and organizing your thoughts, you'll be well on your way to running a successful political campaign. Remember to stay focused, stay motivated, and stay true to your message and goals. Good luck!

www.ingramcontent.com/pod-product-compliance
Lightning Source LLC
Chambersburg PA
CBHW060828260726
48660CB00003B/1150